WORD PLAY

WHO WORDS

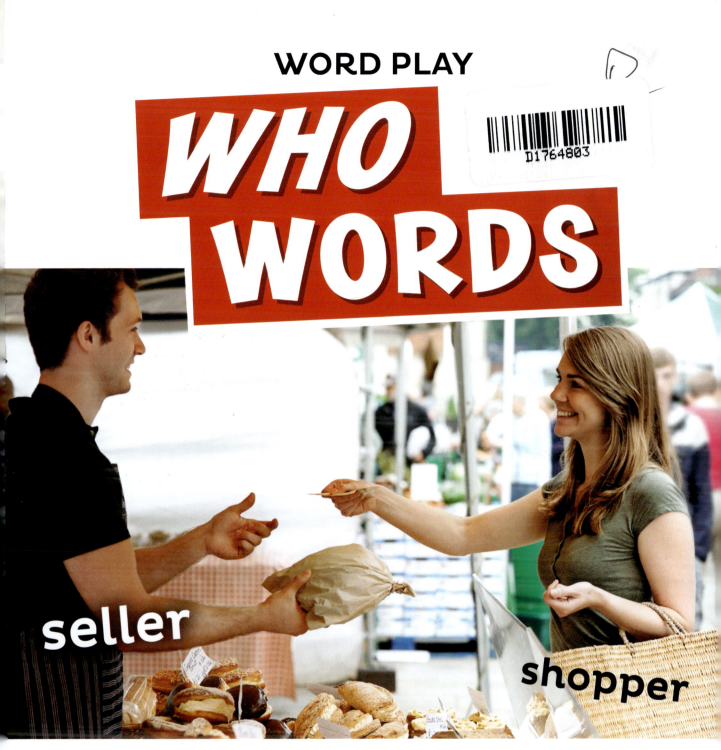

seller

shopper

by Carrie B. Sheely

Who is it?

Is it your friends? Maybe it's the delivery person. Who else could it be? Let words tell you who it is!

delivery person

friends

pals

dad

daddy

father

sister

mother   mum

mummy

brother

grandma

gran

nana

granny

granddaughter

grandson

grandad

grandpa

police officer

paramedics

firefighter

nurse

patient

doctors

teacher

Mr Martin

pupil

pupils

children

librarian

bus
driver

astronaut

space walker

dancers

ballerinas

singer

Taylor Swift

performer

builders

construction workers

bricklayers

road roller driver

swimmers

lifeguard

marine biologist

diver

scientist

vets

animal
trainer

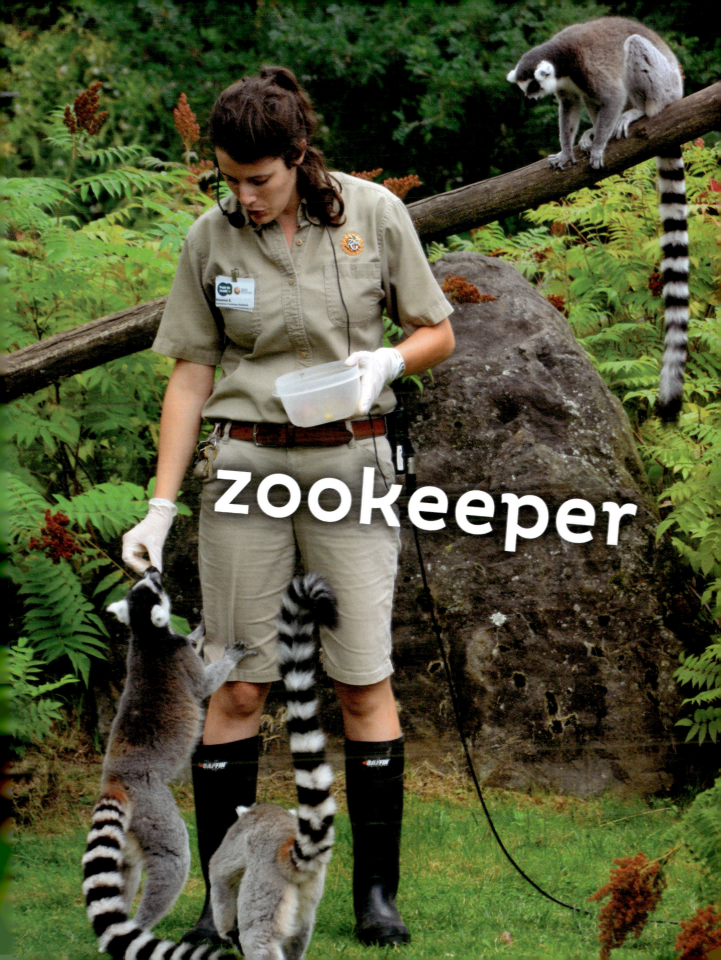

zookeeper

teammates

Emily

Jada

football players

Susie

coach

Simone
Biles

gymnast

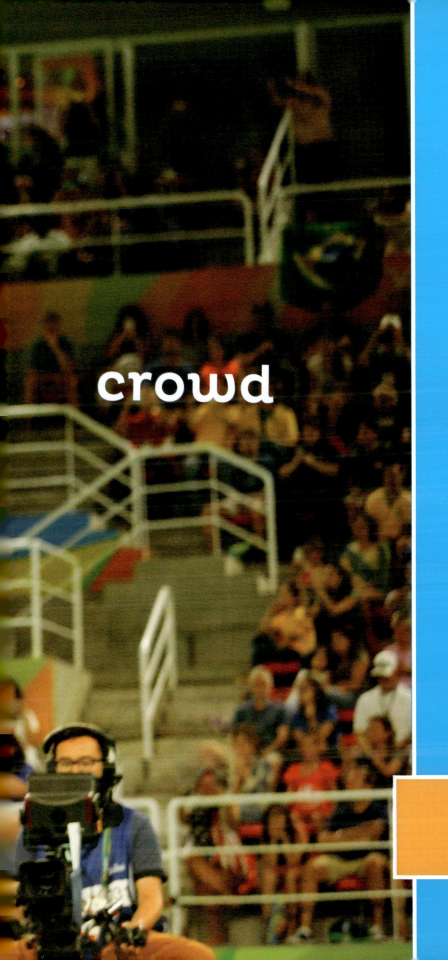

crowd

Who else can you see?

stunt rider

skydiver

climber

players

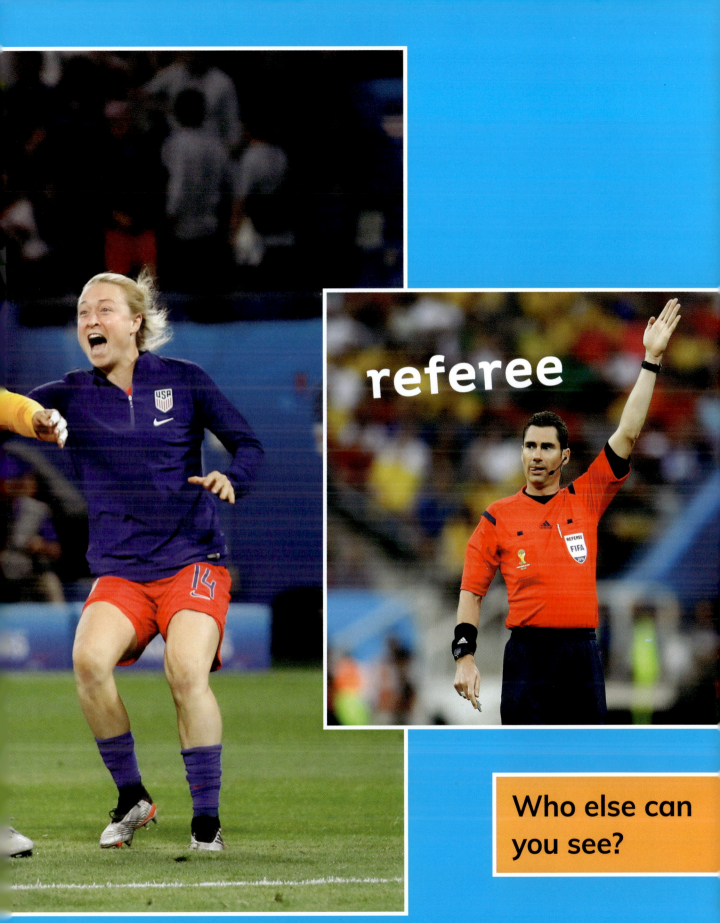

referee

Who else can you see?

Raintree is an imprint of Capstone Global Library Limited, a company incorporated in England and Wales having its registered office at 264 Banbury Road, Oxford, OX2 7DY – Registered company number: 6695582

www.raintree.co.uk
myorders@raintree.co.uk

Designed by Juliette Peters
Picture research by Svetlana Zhurkin
Production by Katy LaVigne

ISBN 978 1 4747 9545 6 (hardback)
ISBN 978 1 4747 9749 8 (paperback)

British Library Cataloguing in Publication Data
A full catalogue record for this book is available from the British Library.

Acknowledgements
We would like to thank the following for permission to reproduce photographs:
Shutterstock: Anastacia Petrova, 18–19 (bottom), Beautiful landscape, 12, Bernie Van Der Vyver, 17, Billy Gadbury, 18 (top), cahya nugraha, 27 (bottom), Cheryl Casey, 21, covenant, 24, Darren Green, 7 (top), denizya, 1, Dmitry Tsvetkov, 10–11, DVAD, 14 (bottom), Ekaterina Kuzovkova, 22 (bottom), Glenn Price, 16 (bottom), Guas, 30–31, HTeam, 28–29, John L. Absher, 13, M. Relova, 14–15, Margarita Borodina, 2–3, Mountains Hunter, 23, Niti Tangpaitoon, 25, Normana Karia, 27 (top), Patrick Reith, 16 (top), Peter_ml, 9, PhotographyByMK, 7 (bottom), Prostock-studio, 20, Richard Whitcombe, 5, Scarc, 22 (top), scoutori, 4, Simon Shim, 8 (top), Susanne Fritzsche, 6, Tetyana Kaganska, 19 (top), topseller, cover, travelwild, 26, Zapfl Cornelia, 8 (bottom)

Every effort has been made to contact copyright holders of material reproduced in this book. Any omissions will be rectified in subsequent printings if notice is given to the publisher.

Titles in this series:

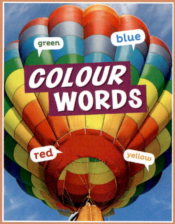

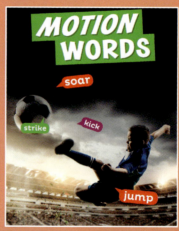

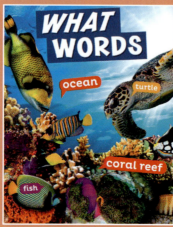